HALLOWEEN HANDBOOK

by Ruth Shannon Odor
Dotti Hannum
Jane Belk Moncure
Penny Anderson
Rosemary Leahy Varney
and others

illustrated by Mina Gow McLean

THE CHILD'S WORLD

ELGIN, ILLINOIS 60120

ASSIGNMENT EDITOR: Diane Dow Suire
EDITORS: Sylvia Root Tester, Sandra Ziegler

Distributed by Childrens Press, 1224 West Van Buren Street, Chicago, Illinois 60607.

Library of Congress Cataloging in Publication Data

Main entry under title:

Halloween handbook.

1. Halloween.   2. Creative activities and seat work.
3. Halloween decorations.   I. Odor, Ruth Shannon, 1926-
GT4965.H33   1984   394.2'683   83-26315
ISBN 0-89565-267-6

1 2 3 4 5 6 7 8 9 10 11 12 R 89 88 87 86 85 84

HALLOWEEN
HANDBOOK

USING
THIS
HANDBOOK

This handbook has been prepared for you if you teach kindergarten through third grade. The ideas in the book can be used in many ways.

You'll be able to choose from assorted stories, poems, songs and a chant, math and science, art and craft, and cooking activities.

Use the ideas for room decorations, bulletin boards, and a party. It will be easy to see it's Halloween in your room.

If you want your children to produce a story play, the section on Costumes and Masks will help.

Halloween is an enjoyable holiday. Have a happy one.

CONTENTS

HOLIDAY HISTORY

by Ruth Shannon Odor

WHO HAD THE FIRST FALL CELEBRATION?

Long ago, some people called Celts believed that on the night of October 31, the spirits of the dead came to earth and roamed about. Spooky! Don't you agree?

These people lived in what is now France, England, Ireland, Scotland, and Wales. October 31 marked the end of their year. At that time, the Celts brought their cattle in from the pastures. They began to eat the first of their winter food supplies. And priests of their religion, Druidism, made sacrifices to their god and to a god called "lord of the dead." This day was called "Samhain," meaning "summer's end."

HOW DID THEY CELEBRATE?

To protect themselves on "Samhain's Eve" (our Halloween), the Celts put out the fires in their homes. They gathered outdoors around altars. First, the Druid priests put out the altar fires. Then they rubbed pieces of oak together and kindled new fires. From the new fires they lit great bonfires on the hilltops. People hoped the fires would scare the ghosts away.

9

Each father was given coals of fire to take home. From these coals he lighted a new fire in his fireplace to drive away any ghosts or spirits he thought might be hiding there.

HOW DID HALLOWEEN GET ITS NAME?

After the Romans began to conquer the Celts, they declared the worship of Druids against the law.

Of course, the Romans also had celebrations in the fall. So gradually their activities were combined with some of the Celts' activities.

Many years later the fall celebration took on new meaning and Halloween came to be.

The Roman Catholic Church decided it should set aside a day for honoring Christians who died for their beliefs. The day the church chose was November 1. People called the day "All Saints' Day," or "All Hallows' Day." Hallow means holy. Just as the evening before Christmas Day is called Christmas Eve, so the evening before All Hallows' Day is called All Hallows' Eve. In time that was shortened to become Halloween.

DID EVERYONE CELEBRATE HALLOWEEN?

No. Not all people were Christians. Some of the non-Christians met on All Hallows' Eve, but they made fun of the church. They celebrated in the old ways. They were called witches.

As time passed, people began to believe that on Halloween, witches flew to meetings on broomsticks. And many people, no matter what their religion, believed Halloween was a time when ghosts and goblins might harm people.

People met together on All Hallows' Eve, so they wouldn't be so scared. They munched apples and nuts, told each other ghost stories, and played games such as bobbing for apples.

In many rural areas groups of merrymakers, dressed up and wearing masks, played tricks on their neighbors. They covered chimneys, blocked doorways, and stole gates.

"They'll think the ghosts did it," said the merrymakers, laughing.

And sometimes, people did think ghosts were responsible.

WHY DO WE CELEBRATE HALLOWEEN AS WE DO?

The people who first settled America did not celebrate Halloween at all. They thought it was not a Christian thing to do.

Later, some Americans did hold taffy pulls, corn poppings, hayrides, Snap-Apple Nights, or Nutcracker Nights on October 31. It was almost the end of harvest and getting together was fun.

But it was when Irish people came to America to escape the great Irish potato famine, that the traditional ways to celebrate All Hallows' Eve were introduced. These ways, of course, they had learned from their parents who had learned them from theirs, and so on, clear back to All Hallows' Eve and even to the days when the Druid priests were lighting bonfires. Many of the things we do to celebrate the day are things the Irish did.

Today Halloween is no longer a time of fear and superstition. It is a time to think of cookies, apples, and candy; jack-o'-lanterns, costumes, and masks; parties, carnivals, and "trick or treat." It is a time of laughter and fun.

BEFORE THE RUSH

by Ruth Shannon Odor

Begin your preparations for Halloween early. Avoid that last-minute rush. Here are some ideas to help you and your students enjoy the Halloween season.

CLASSROOM CALENDAR

Make a large classroom calendar of things to do for the month of October. For the background, use a large sheet of orange posterboard (usually about 22" × 28"). From white, black, or green paper, cut 31 2½-inch squares, one for each day in October. Print the numbers of the days of the month on these squares. Around the numbers, draw owls, bats, cats, pumpkins, and ghosts.

Tape or glue only the top of each number square to the calendar, so each "day" can be lifted up. (You should have about 1½ inches on each side of the calendar area and ¼ inch between each row of squares.) Underneath each flap write a task the children can do to help get ready for Halloween. Each day check the calendar for the day's task. This will involve the children and keep preparations moving.

STORY TIME

Choose one story, or several, to read to your students during the month of October. On pages 82-96, you can find two classic English folk tales—"The Old Witch" and "Teeny-Tiny,"— and two modern stories—"Laurie Hated Halloween" and "Wispy, the Littlest Witch."

Illustrated here are several suitable books available from *The Child's World.*

THE PUMPKIN

Plan a unit of study on the pumpkin. Investigate how pumpkins grow, ways people use them, and the nutritional value of pumpkins. Try to visit a pumpkin patch. Compare them by size—big, little. Guess a pumpkin's weight.

For a math activity, count the seeds in a pumpkin, then put them into sets of five.

Older children might like to estimate how many new pumpkins could be grown from the seeds of one pumpkin. Students would need to find out how many seeds are in the pumpkin, how many of these seeds would be likely to sprout, and how many of the sprouts would be likely to grow.

Art, music, and oral or written activities could also be based upon the pumpkin. See page 54 for additional ideas.

HARVEST TIME

For older pupils plan a unit of study on harvest time. Invite a senior citizen who grew up on a farm to come and talk to your students. Ask your guest if he might like to wear the kind of clothing he or she once wore for farm work.

Ask your guest to talk about how crops were harvested in his or her youth, about how farmers got together to help each other at harvest time, and about how wives fixed huge harvest meals for the workers.

Tie in this information with a study of modern harvesting techniques.

AUTUMN EMPHASIS

With younger students, talk about the changing seasons. Go for a nature walk. Bring back items that show the change in seasons— colorful leaves, seed pods, nuts, etc. Talk about the ways people know summer is gone and winter is coming—the weather changes, birds migrate, grasses and weeds brown and die, seeds scatter, mammals grow winter fur, etc.

ROOM DECORATIONS

Since October is usually the month leaves change colors and drop, students might like to bring in beautiful leaves to make a display.

Cornstalks and pumpkins can also be used to make a colorful harvest display. You'll find a wealth of other decorating ideas for your classroom on pages 18-24.

PLAN A HALLOWEEN PARTY

Let students come in costumes. Ask a parent with a dramatic flair to visit your class and tell a story or give a reading about Halloween. (Of course, the parent should come "dressed" for his topic!) See pages 49-52 for additional suggestions.

PRODUCE A PLAY

You will want to read over the suggested activities on pages 58 and 59 and the story of Wispy on page 91. Children enjoy dressing up in costumes and putting on plays. The story of Wispy lends itself to dramatization. Let the girls be witches and boys be black cats.

You may want to give this some thought and develop some lists of things you need to do. Your advance planning will help you when you begin to lead the children in planning their production.

A Reminder: For religious reasons some parents wish to exclude their children from Halloween activities. Since this might be true of parents of your students, make alternative plans ahead of time so those students won't feel ostracized or excluded.

Those students can be included, of course, in the activities that stress the changing seasons, and in many other traditional autumn activities.

With older students, discuss the issues of freedom of religion and respect for other people's beliefs with the entire class.

HALLOWEEN AROUND THE ROOM

ROOM DECORATIONS

HANGING WITCHES

Materials: 9" × 12" black construction paper, 3" black circles, string, assorted paper scraps, white glue and/or tape, scissors, crayons.

1. Show the children how to fold paper cones. First have them fold one corner of the paper over so the outside edges meet.

2. Tie the ends of a piece of string together.

3. Place the string on the paper so it runs along the inside edge of the piece you folded over and the loop is on the side with the fold.

4. Fold the bottom flap up over the string. Be sure the edges opposite the fold line up. Glue down.

5. Fold the flap back over the folded edge and glue it down.

6. Draw and cut an arc off at the bottom opposite the point. Save the piece you cut off.

7. With flap to the back, place the flattened cone on the desk. Cut a triangle from a scrap and draw face for the witch with crayons. Glue on. Use a three-inch black circle cut in the center as in the sketch to make the hat. Slip it over her head. (Show the children a completed sample.)

8. Cut arms from the scrap which is left. (See the sketch.)

9. Tell the children they may create and add brooms or cats to their witches' hands.

—*by Sandra Ziegler*

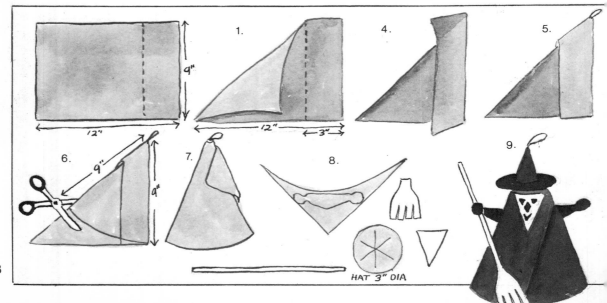

STRIP PUMPKIN

Materials: four orange paper strips (approximately 1½" wide and 8" long), green and black paper (large scraps will do), paste or glue, scissors, string, stapler.

1. Ask students to glue strips one on top of the other to form a pattern as in sketch.

2. While glue sets, cut jack-o'-lantern features from the black paper. Cut a one-inch circle and stem from green paper.

3. Turn paper strips over. Place drop of glue on end of each strip. Glue one on top of the other to form pumpkin.

4. Glue face and stem on strips.

5. Staple or tie string at top. Hang from ceiling.

—by Dotti Hannum

PUMPKIN FACES

Here is an activity to help provide practice in recognizing shapes.

Materials: For each child, a pumpkin shape cut from orange construction paper. (Use pattern on this page.) Lots of squares, circles, triangles, rectangles, and ovals, cut from black construction paper; paste.

Give each child a pumpkin shape. Let each child choose black shapes and paste them on the pumpkin to make a face. Talk about the shapes. Encourage students to name the shapes.

WINDOW WATCHERS

Materials: black, white, or cream construction paper, crayons, scissors, glue, orange or yellow tissue paper, masking tape.

1. Let students draw large cat, ghost, or bat eyes on construction paper.

2. Around the eyes, let students draw the rest of the cat head or bat or ghost. (Show samples you have drawn ahead of time, as you explain the project.)

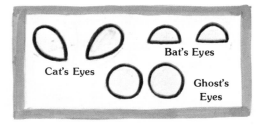

3. Place two sheets of paper together and cut out the figure. Cut out the eyes on each piece. Glue orange or yellow tissue paper behind the eyes on one sheet. Glue the two figures together so the eyes line up. Tape the picture to the window, so the light shines "through" the eyes.

4. From construction paper, make letters to spell, "Whooo sees you?" and tape the letters to the window.

Whooo...
is reading our
spook stories?

Pam ✓   Tanya
John   Kathy ✓✓
Mary ✓   Sue
Angelo
Tony
Harry ✓
Peter ✓✓

OWL POSTER

Place a special Halloween poster in the reading area. Put selected Halloween books on a table or shelf nearby. Tell the students that as they finish reading the books they should write their names on the poster. If the students finish more than one book, they may add checks after their names, one for each additional book they read.

Use a paper grocery bag to make an owl for your poster. Follow the steps shown in the illustrations. Fasten the owl to the poster board and print this sentence: "Who-o-o is reading our spooky stories?"

Leave space below the caption for students to put their names.

1

Make eyes from construction paper, beak from corner cut from bag (see illustration two).

Glue face on bottom of bag.

Stuff a bit of paper in bottom to give owl some depth. Fold back down.

MOUTH   EARS

CUT

2

Cut off two corners from bottom of bag. Draw wings.

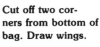

CUT

3

Tape corners from bottom of bag to the sides of head as tufts. Stuff some paper inside and glue closed. Glue owl on poster.

22

HALLOWEEN BULLETIN BOARDS

DARK SHADOWS

Materials: white paper, a desk lamp or flashlight, items to display —ball, block, doll, rag, and others as you have them, black and orange crayons.

1. Cover the bulletin board with white paper.

2. At the upper right corner, attach a bright lamp or light. A desk lamp with a clamp would be ideal. A flashlight could be used instead.

3. Attach various objects to the bulletin board, such as a ball, a block, a doll, and an old rag.

4. Let a student turn on the light and draw a silhouette outline at the edges of the shadow of an object. Student may use black crayon. Repeat for each item.

5. Compare the shapes of the objects with the shapes of the shadows.

6. Move the light to the bottom right corner. Let students draw new silhouette outlines of the shadows, this time with orange crayons. Compare and contrast the outlines.

EERIE OWL'S
HALLOWEEN WORDS

Materials: construction paper, crayons, scissors. For students—drawing paper and crayons, tape or thumbtacks.

1. Make an "Eerie Owl" from construction paper, similar to the owl shown below. Attach the owl to the upper left corner of the bulletin board.

2. Add the caption: "Eerie Owl's Halloween Words."

3. Ask the students to draw pictures of Halloween objects and characters. The students should label their pictures. (For younger students, you will need to label the pictures.)

4. Attach the pictures to the bulletin board.

5. If some of your students are bilingual, label the pictures in English and in the language your bilingual students speak. This will help your bilingual students learn some new English words, while your English-speaking students learn some new foreign words.

HALLOWEEN IN THE LEARNING CENTERS

LEARNING CENTERS

by Ruth Shannon Odor

STORY PUMPKIN

Fill a plastic or paper pumpkin with slips of paper. Each slip should have the title of a possible Halloween story on it. Let each student reach inside the pumpkin, take out a piece of paper, read the title, and write a story about it.

Younger children might work in small groups to make up a story about a single title or picture you have placed in the pumpkin in advance. An aide could help the group write the story. Or you might let pupils draw picture stories about their subjects and tell them to you.

HERE ARE SOME TITLES:

"Michael and the Monster"

"The Midnight Meeting"
"Brian and the Haunted House"
"The Ghost of Oaktown"
"When the Clock Struck Twelve"
"The Haunted House on High Street"
"The Pumpkin Patch"
"The Laughing Ghost"
"The Mysterious Stranger"
"Jody's Jack-o'-Lantern"
"The Halloween Party"
"The Mask and the Monster"
"The Friendly Ghost"
"The Mysterious Black Cat"

If you prefer, suggest subjects instead of titles. Here are a few to get you going: a haunted house, a laughing ghost, pumpkins, a black cat, a monster.

STORY PUMPKIN

Reach inside me;
I won't bite.
Find a story,
You can write.

SOUNDS OF HALLOWEEN

1. Push "Start."
2. Listen to the sound.
3. Push "Stop."
4. Write what the sound is.
5. Keep doing steps 1-4 over again until you have heard all ten sounds.
6. Give your paper to the teacher.

SOUNDS OF HALLOWEEN

Before Halloween, tape sounds associated with the season on a cassette recorder. Allow a pause between each sound.

Include some or all of these sounds: a shriek, chains clanging, wind howling, footsteps, a door opening, shutters banging, a ghost laughing, a ghost moaning, an owl screeching, a cat meowing. (You should be able to find these sounds and others on a sound effects recording in a nearby library.)

To set up the listening center, place the cassette recorder and tape on a table. Provide some pencils and paper. Fasten an instruction sheet to the wall nearby or place a cardboard sign on an easel near the cassette recorder. (If you don't have headphones, place this center away from other activities.)

Let each student have a chance to visit the center. Let him listen to each sound, identify it, and write down what it is. Kindergarten and first grade children would enjoy listening. They could tell a teacher or aide what sounds they hear.

MONSTER MADNESS

What adult does not remember a time when he watched the shadows play on the walls of a dark bedroom and thought of monsters? Halloween is a good time to explore such fears with your children. Help them realize that others have fears just as they do.

Set aside a display area where each child can display a monster he has created. Lead into the activity with a discussion.

Explore the answers to these suggested questions: "Did you ever think you saw a monster?" "How did you feel?" "What did your monster look like?" "Do all monsters look alike?" "How are they alike?" "How are they different?" "If you could be a monster, what kind would you be?"

Direct the attention of the class to some monster books. Good titles you might want to use include: *What Is a Monster? Magic Monsters' Halloween, Learning About Monsters* (see page 14). Suggest that each child look over the books. Then he will want to plan a visit to the Monster Center where he may make a clay model of his idea of the perfect monster. Ask an aide to help each child prepare a sign to go with his monster. His sign should identify the monster and tell what it is. Display the monsters and the labels.

THE SPIDER'S WEB

In advance, make a "spider's web;" use it to motivate learning in spelling or math. To make the web, first place an × over a + with string. Insert push pins into a cork board in a pattern similar to the one illustrated. Then wrap string over and around the pins to create the web. Be sure children can reach it.

Make a large spider from construction paper or use a Halloween spider cut-out. Put him outside the web along with the caption: "Who's That in My Web?" Make small spiders from the pattern here.

Each time a child gets all his spelling words or math problems right, let him put a spider into the web.

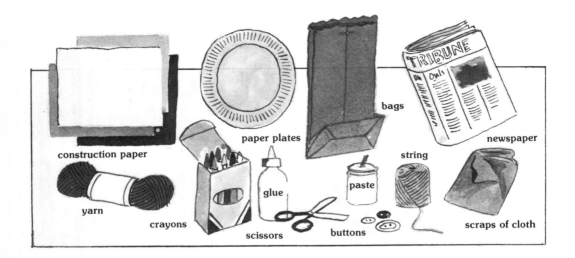

construction paper

paper plates

bags

newspaper

yarn

crayons

glue

scissors

paste

buttons

string

scraps of cloth

HALLOWEEN ART CENTER

Set up a table with a variety of art supplies. Include crayons, paste and glue, scissors, and lots of construction paper. In addition, provide yarn, paper bags, paper plates, newspaper, scraps of cloth, buttons, string, and anything else you have available.

In a box or bag, place a number of art assignments. Let each student choose an assignment he likes and do it. Here are a few possible assignments.

1. Make a Halloween mask.

2. Make a scary scene. Use a piece of black paper for the background. Cut figures, trees, and houses from newspaper. Paste these on the black paper.

3. Make a haunted house.

4. Draw two Halloween witches and decorate their dresses. Make them very different from each other.

5. Make a "fat cat."

6. Cut construction paper into tiny pieces. Use the tiny pieces to make a Halloween face.

7. Make a huge monster.

8. Make a scarecrow.

9. From a paper plate, cut eye and mouth holes to make a mask. Glue yarn on the face, making fancy patterns with the yarn.

HALLOWEEN
RESEARCH CENTER

Set up a research center in a quiet area of the room. Choose three to four Halloween topics, such as ghosts, cats, bats, owls, witches, or mummies. Supply simple books that contain information about the topics you have chosen.

For each topic you choose, write three to seven questions on a large sheet of paper. The age and ability of your students will determine the kinds of questions you ask. Be sure students can find the answers to the questions in the books that are provided. Tape the papers to the wall above the books.

Also provide pencils and paper. Let students choose a topic, research it by searching for the answers in the books, and then write out answers to the questions.

This is a good activity for students who finish their regular work early.

ABOUT OWLS

1. Can owls see in the daytime?

2. Where do screech owls make their nests?

3. What kind of owl lives in a cactus?

The Owl in the Attic

OWLS

BLACK CATS

Invite a black cat to visit the classroom accompanied by someone from the humane society, a veterinarian, or its adult owner.

In advance read the section about cats as symbols on page 63. Talk with the children about whether they think black cats cause bad luck. Explain how such superstitions might have come to be. Point out that while witches and ghosts may be scary and are make-believe, black cats are real and usually friendly. They just get bad press. Let the children ask questions they may have about black cats. The children would also enjoy reading or hearing cat stories.

After the cat is gone, set up a center where students can come to make black cats from construction paper. See directions below.

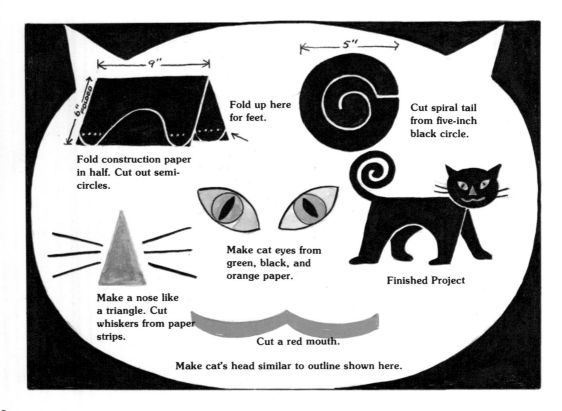

9"
6" folded
Fold up here for feet.
Fold construction paper in half. Cut out semi-circles.

5"
Cut spiral tail from five-inch black circle.

Finished Project

Make cat eyes from green, black, and orange paper.

Make a nose like a triangle. Cut whiskers from paper strips.

Cut a red mouth.

Make cat's head similar to outline shown here.

HALLOWEEN GAMES AND RHYTHMIC ACTIVITIES

HALLOWEEN ACTION RHYMES

by Jane Belk Moncure and Dotti Hannum

HALLOWEEN FINGER PLAY

(Let children hold up ten fingers for the first verse, nine fingers for the next verse, and so on, through the ten verses.)

Ten Jack-o'-lanterns,
   My! How they shine!
Out goes one candle;
   Now there are nine.

Nine spooky goblins
   Swinging on a gate.
One jumps off!
   Now there are eight.

Eight little monsters
   Sitting on a hill.
One stands up,
   Leaving seven sitting still.

Seven magic ghosts
   Do Halloween tricks.
One disappears;
   Now there are six.

Six chocolate cats
  Look quite alive.
One goes "trick or treating;"
  Now there are five.

Five funny skeletons
  Hide behind a door.
One hops away;
  Now there are four.

Four howling owls
  Hooting in a tree.
One flies away;
  Now there are three.

Three wacky witches
  Making up a stew.
One flies away;
  Now there are two.

Two scary spacemen
  March and skip and run.
One climbs into a ship;
  Now there is one.

One robot rides a rocket
  Looking for some fun.
But the rocket zooms away;
  So now there are none!

CAT AND GHOST

I saw a big black cat.
  (Hold hands out at shoulder level.)
I saw a bigger one too.
  (Hold hands just above head.)
I saw a great big black cat,
  (Stretch hands very high.)
And heard it say, "Mew."
  (Say, "Mew.")

I saw a great big ghost,
  (Lower hands just above head.)
I saw a smaller one too.
  (Lower hands to shoulder level.)
I saw a tiny little ghost.
  (Stoop down.)
And heard it say, "Boo!"
  (Shout, "Boo!" Jump up.)

LEARNING GAMES

Selected Ideas to Try

MISS THE PUMPKIN

(Physical Education and Math)

In a gym or outside, place two small pumpkins two feet apart. Chalk a line on the floor six feet in front of the pumpkins. Let each student in turn stand behind the line and try to roll a ball between the two pumpkins, not touching either one. The children may divide into teams and keep count of the number of times they succeed.

GHOSTS AND WITCHES
(Physical Education and Music)

Let the boys be ghosts and the girls be witches. Use some spooky Halloween music for this activity. Have the girls form an inside circle, the boys an outside circle around

students skip. Then play very fast music and let the students run. Go back to skipping music and finally to the walking music.

ON HALLOWEEN NIGHT
(Physical Education and Music)

Divide the children into small groups: cats, bats, witches, ghosts,

them. Pair off the children so that all have partners. Then ask the girls to turn and face one direction, the boys the other.

As the music begins, each circle will revolve the direction it is facing. When the music stops, let the ghosts and witches find their original partners, join hands with them, and stoop down.

After walking a few times, play livelier Halloween music and let the

owls, monsters, and so forth.

Tell the children to listen for their group names and movements, and then do them.

Play some Halloween music and begin to ad lib as you give directions: "It was Halloween night, dark and clear, when the flying bats began to appear. . ." Other instructions: witches marched, ghosts skipped, cats jumped, owls swooped, and so forth.

HALLOWEEN ACTION POEM

by Dotti Hannum

Materials: six large sheets of construction paper, orange paper, markers, scissors, glue.

Ahead of time, make four jack-o'-lanterns from orange paper: one happy, one sad, one sleepy, and one angry. Paste each on a separate sheet of construction paper.

Cut small pieces of orange paper and paste these on a fifth sheet. Make a picture of a pumpkin pie, cut it out, and paste it on the sixth sheet.

Write one line of the poem on each sheet, below the illustration.

Choose six children to help you. Give each one a sheet to hold. Then teach the action poem.

This is Jack-o'-Happy.
 (Children smile.)
This is Jack-o'-Sad.
 (Children look sad, pretend to cry.)
This is Jack-o'-Sleepy.
 (Children close eyes.)
This is Jack-o'-Mad.
 (Children stomp feet, shake fists.)
This is Jack in pieces small.
In a pumpkin pie, he's best of all!
 (Children rub tummies.)

1 This is JACK-O'-HAPPY

2 This is JACK-O'-SAD

3 This is JACK-O'-SLEEPY

4 This is JACK-O'-MAD

5 This is JACK in pieces small...

6 ...in a pumpkin pie, he's best of all.

HALLOWEEN THINGS TO MAKE AND DO

ART AND CRAFT ACTIVITIES
by Dotti Hannum

HALLOWEEN PLACE MATS

Materials: 12" × 18" orange construction paper, crayons, scissors.

1. Draw and color Halloween pictures on the 12" × 18" sheets of paper. Children may draw ghosts, witches, cats, or bats.

2. Fringe the edges by cutting slits about 3/4" into the mat all around the edges.

3. Each child might like to make one place mat for each member of his or her family.

MUSLIN OR TISSUE GHOST

Materials: small squares or rectangles of muslin or white facial tissues, string cut in 6" lengths, black markers.

1. Find the center of the muslin or tissue.

2. Stuff this center section with paper or another tissue. This will form ghost's head.

3. Tie with a string under the "head."

4. Draw eyes and a mouth with black markers or paint and brush.

A HALLOWEEN PAINTING

Material: white poster paint, big primary paint brushes, 12" × 18" black paper, orange construction paper, scissors, glue or paste, cover-ups or aprons for students.

Let your students follow these directions.

1. Use white poster paint to paint any Halloween symbol on black paper. Some possible symbols are a cat, a ghost, a witch, a monster, a bat, a vampire, bare tree branches, a haunted house, or an owl. Use large sheets of paper and wide primary brushes to make the paintings large and effective.

2. Let paint dry.

3. From orange paper cut accents, such as orange eyes, or windows, or a slice of moon. Add these to the painting. Just this little bit of color adds a lot.

WITCH OF SHAPES

Materials: black and orange or green construction paper, scissors, glue, yarn, crayons.

1. From black construction paper, cut two different sizes of triangles to make the witch's body. Cut smaller triangles for the witch's hat and head.

2. Also from the black paper, cut thin rectangles about 6" long to make the witch's arms and legs.

3. From orange or green paper, cut a square about 1-5/8" to make the witch's face.

4. Glue the shapes together to form the witch's body. Glue yarn pieces on for hair. Draw features. Add shoes, a black cat, etc.

SKELETON

Materials: white and black construction paper, glue or paste, scissors, black crayons.

Ahead of time, make a skeleton to use as an example for the children. If you have a real skeleton or a chart showing human bone structure, display this as well.

1. Cut white paper into strips of different lengths or widths.

2. Paste white strips on black paper to form the bones. Leave spaces between the bones.

3. Cut out and glue on a white skull.

4. Draw the eye sockets and teeth with black crayon.

PAPER BAG PUMPKIN

Materials: paper bags, newspapers, string, green, orange, and black tempera paint, brushes, black construction paper, scissors, glue or paste.

1. Stuff a paper bag with newspaper.

2. Tie the top closed with string.

3. To make the stem, paint the bag green above the the string.

4. Paint the rest of bag orange. Let paint dry.

5. Paint jack-o'-lantern features on the orange portion, using black paint. Or, cut features from black construction paper and glue them onto the pumpkin.

PAPER BAG OWL

Materials: small brown paper bags, black, white, brown, and orange construction paper, glue or paste.

For younger students, ahead of time, cut out many white circles about 1½" in diameter. Cut many black circles about ½" in diameter. Cut many black triangles. From the brown and orange paper, cut a sup-

ply of "snippets" of paper (to use as owl feathers). Let older students cut parts themselves.

1. Paste two white circles on the bottom of the bag for eyes.

2. Paste two black circles inside the white circles.

3. Paste a black triangle on the bottom of the bag, for a beak.

4. Paste tiny paper "snippets" on sides of bag for owl's feathers.

Paint stem green

Paint bag orange

Flap

ART AND LANGUAGE-ARTS ACTIVITIES

by Dotti Hannum

TOBY'S HOUSE

Materials: orange paper, scissors.

(This is a Halloween story to tell to your students, as you make Toby's house. Then students may make Toby's house themselves, as you retell the story.)

Once upon a time, there was a little boy named Toby. Toby was six years old. He had a pet mouse named Petey.

One day Toby and Petey went for a walk. They walked in the woods. It was a cool day in autumn, and as they walked along, they saw many pretty leaves on the trees.

"This would be a good place to build a house," said Toby. "When I'm not in school, we could come and watch the pretty leaves fall to the ground."

Petey thought that was a splendid idea. "What kind of a house shall we build?" asked Petey.

"Let's make a round house," said Toby.

Fold paper in half. Then cut a half circle.

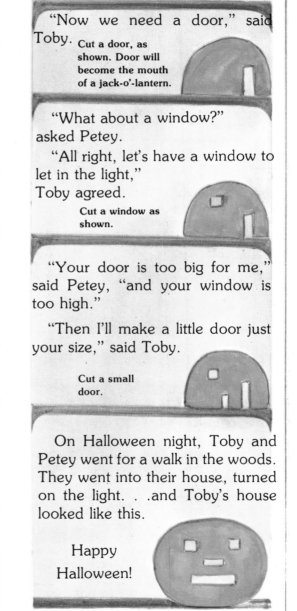

"Now we need a door," said Toby. Cut a door, as shown. Door will become the mouth of a jack-o'-lantern.

"What about a window?" asked Petey.

"All right, let's have a window to let in the light," Toby agreed.

Cut a window as shown.

"Your door is too big for me," said Petey, "and your window is too high."

"Then I'll make a little door just your size," said Toby.

Cut a small door.

On Halloween night, Toby and Petey went for a walk in the woods. They went into their house, turned on the light. . .and Toby's house looked like this.

Happy Halloween!

44

WIDE-EYED OWL

Materials: pencils, paper, crayons.

(This is a Halloween poem to recite as you draw an owl. Then let students draw their own owls as you recite the poem again.)

I know a wide-eyed owl

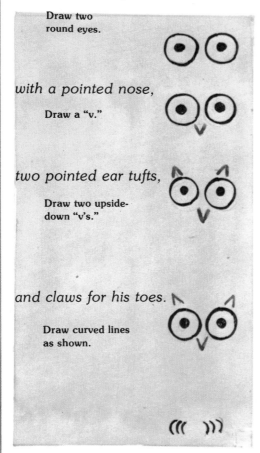

Draw two round eyes.

with a pointed nose,

Draw a "v."

two pointed ear tufts,

Draw two upside-down "v's."

and claws for his toes.

Draw curved lines as shown.

He lives high in a tree.

Draw tree branch as shown.

When he looks at you,

Draw tail just below tree branch.

he flaps his wings

Draw wings as shown. Then add feathers.

and says, "Ooooooooooooh."

Draw in rest of head.

MASKS AND COSTUMES

by Ruth Shannon Odor and Dotti Hannum

PAPER BAG MASKS

Materials: brown paper bags of medium size, scissors, pencils, crayons or felt pens, construction paper, paste or glue, crepe paper.

Give each person a brown paper grocery bag that is large enough to slip over a child's head. Use scissors, to split the folds in the bag at the four open corners so it will slip over the child's head. With a pencil, mark lightly the location of eyes, nose, and mouth. Remove bag. Cut holes for the eyes, nose, and mouth.

Now the student is ready to work on his own. Tell students to draw a face on the masks, using crayons or felt pens. Then students can decorate the masks with colored construction paper. Finally, they can add crepe-paper hair, construction-paper hats, or other features.

When the decorating is finished, cut the bottom of each mask to fit below the child's chin.

Bird

Turtle

HALLOWEEN CREATURES

Materials: poster board, construction paper, colored markers, scissors, string, chenille wire, stapler.

1. You will want to cut two large round circles for each person. Each child may decorate one side of each of his circles with markers or construction paper: spots/ladybug, shell markings/turtle, paper feathers/bird, and so forth.

2. Fasten at the top like a sandwich board.

3. Suggest that students wear dark shirts and pants underneath.

4. "Bugs" may cut eye masks and add chenille-wire feelers. Others may need to make appropriate paper bag masks.

WITCH HATS

Materials: a section of newspaper for each student, black crayons, or black paint and brushes, stapler, scissors, orange construction paper, paste.

1. For each student, cut a large half-circle from a section (6 to 8 pages) of newspaper.

2. Let students paint one side of their half-circles black.

3. Fringe the rounded edge.

4. Form half-circle into a cone. Adjust size and staple to fit child's head.

5. Let students finish their hats by decorating them with orange moons or pumpkins.

COOKING ACTIVITIES
Ideas from Several Sources

APPLESAUCE

1. Ask each child to bring an apple to class. You will also need sugar, a lemon, and several cinnamon sticks. Be prepared to cook the applesauce on a stove or hot plate in a large soup pot or in an electric cooker.

2. Let students help you quarter, core, and slice the apples. If you plan to use a sieve, do not peel the apples. Teach students the safe way to use a knife or peeler.

3. Put apples in a pot. Slice and add lemon, peel and all. Add some water.

4. Bring mixture to a boil. Let cook a few minutes. Add cinnamon sticks. Cook until apples are soft and falling apart. Add sugar, about one cup per 10 apples. Remove cinnamon. Put through sieve.

HALLOWEEN FACES TO EAT

Materials: cheese cubes, raw vegetables cut in strips, slices, and squares, raisins, nuts, orange paper plates.

Provide a selection of food for each student. Let students form the food into Halloween faces, then eat the food.

TOASTED PUMPKIN SEEDS

Materials: pumpkin seeds from jack-o'-lantern, foil, oil, cookie sheet, salt, bowl, oven or toaster oven, spoons.

After you carve your jack-o'-lantern, save the seeds to make a special treat. Let your students help you with every step of the process.

1. Wash the seeds thoroughly. Then soak the seeds about an hour.

2. Spread the seeds on foil to dry. (Foil prevents sticking.) Let dry for a day or two.

3. Place seeds in a bowl and pour in a teaspoon or two of cooking oil. Stir seeds to distribute oil.

4. Spread seeds out on a large cookie sheet.

5. Salt seeds.

6. Bake at 300° for about 30 minutes, turning the seeds every five minutes.

HOLD A HALLOWEEN PARTY

by Ruth Shannon Odor

DECORATIONS

If the party is held in the classroom, most of the decorations already will be there. (See pages 18-24.) You may want to add cornstalks in a corner of the room, a large jack-o'-lantern, autumn leaves, and orange and black crepe-paper streamers.

GAMES

Choose from the following.

Mind Reading. For this game, the teacher (the mind reader) will need an accomplice who understands the trick. If a parent or aide is helping with the party, he or she can be the accomplice. Otherwise, ask a student, or perhaps two, to help.

The idea of the game is to pretend you are able to tell what number students are thinking of, by looking into their eyes.

The mind reader goes out of the room. Students choose a number. For younger students, use a figure between one and nine. Older students could use a number to 99.

The mind reader is brought back to the room and goes from student to student. The teacher lays his or her hands on each person's cheeks so that the hands cover the jaw bones. Then the teacher looks into the person's eyes. The player is to "think hard about the number."

When the mind reader comes to the accomplice, the accomplice bites his jaws together just enough to allow the mind reader to feel the jaw bones moving. If the number is six, the accomplice bites six times. If the number is 25, the accomplice bites two times, pauses, then bites five times. The teacher will be wise to go to several students after going to the accomplice, and then to "guess" the number.

Afterward, explain that you have pulled a trick, and see if the students can guess how you did it.

Witch's Hunt. Before the party, cut figures of cats, bats, owls, and pumpkins out of cardboard or construction paper. Hide these around the room.

Play spooky music as the children march around in a circle. When the music stops, the players try to find as many cats, bats, owls, and pumpkins as they can.

You may use the music only once; or you may have the players return to the circle when the music starts, and hunt again when the music stops.

Assign points to each figure. Bats might count as one point each, cats as two, owls as three, and pumpkins as five. Let each student add up his or her points. The person with the most points wins. (But not with younger students.)

Halloween Costume Relay. Children stand in two equal lines at one end of the room. At the other end of the room, place two chairs. On each chair, place a Halloween costume—jacket, skirt, mask. Keep the costumes simple. Each child runs to the chair, puts on the costume, takes a bow, takes off the costume, returns it to the chair, runs back, and touches the next player. The first team finished wins.

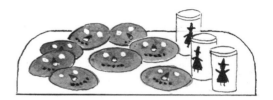

The Ghost and His Statues. Each student stands as still as a statue in any pose demanded by the Ghost. No one is allowed to laugh. The Ghost then tries to get the players to laugh. The Ghost may put on funny Halloween masks, or make faces, or tell jokes. When a person laughs, he is out of the game. (For younger students, provide an alternate activity. Or, let the one who laughs become the Ghost. Many younger students have not learned how to lose gracefully yet.)

Ghostly Snowball Relay. Divide students into two teams. The first player on each team is blindfolded. He carries a cotton ball in a spoon to a container at the opposite end of the room, drops the ball into the container, and returns to give the spoon to the next player. At the end, the team with the most balls in its container wins.

"Who-o-o!" Says the Wise Old Owl. The children stand in a circle. One student becomes "It" and is blindfolded and turned around several times in center circle. When "It" feels sure he is standing in front of someone, he asks, "Who are you?"

That player must anwer, "Who-o-o," but he can disguise his voice, making it shrill, deep, loud, soft, or an imitation of an owl. If "It" recognizes the player's voice, then that player becomes "It."

Alphabet Ghost Story. Ask students to sit in a circle. Give each child a piece of paper on which is written one letter of the alphabet. The leader (teacher or helper) sits in the center of the circle and begins to tell or read a ghost story. At different points in the story, the leader stops and points to a child, who must supply a word beginning with the letter he is holding.

REFRESHMENTS

For refreshments, serve orange punch, and chocolate cupcakes or jack-o'-lantern cookies. To make the cookies, frost plain round cookies with orange frosting. Add raisins to make the eyes, nose, and mouth.

(Also see page 48 for other Halloween food ideas.)

HALLOWEEN IN TRADITIONS AND SYMBOLS

THE JACK-O'-LANTERN

by Ruth Shannon Odor

BACKGROUND

Can you even imagine a jack-o'-lantern made out of something besides a pumpkin? The first jack-o'-lanterns were made from potatoes, turnips, or rutabagas. Irish children hollowed out the vegetables, carved ugly faces on them, put candles inside, and carried the vegetables as lanterns at Halloween.

An old Irish folktale tells how these "lanterns" came to be called jack-o'-lanterns. The story is not true, of course, but it is funny.

Jack and the Devil

Once there lived a man named Jack. Jack was the stingiest man around. What is worse, Jack liked to get drunk. And when he was drunk, he was even stingier.

One evening, Jack was drinking at the local bar. The Devil came.

"It's time to come with me," said the Devil.

"Let's have a drink together," Jack said, "and then I'll go."

The Devil nodded. "But you have to pay for the drink."

Jack looked in his pocket. He didn't have any money either. "Tell you what," he said. "You can change yourself into any shape you want. Change yourself into a coin. I'll use it to buy our drinks. Then you can change yourself back."

The Devil agreed. He changed himself into a bright, shiny coin. Jack snatched it up and put it in his wallet—a wallet with a picture of a cross on it.

"Let me out! Let me out!" the Devil screamed. He twisted and turned inside the wallet, but he was trapped inside.

"I'll make a deal with you," said Jack. "Give me one more year on earth, and I'll let you out."

The Devil agreed.

One year later, the Devil came back. Once more, Jack tricked the Devil who again went home alone.

Not long after that, Jack died.

Jack was so mean he couldn't get into heaven. So he again faced the Devil.

"I don't want you causing trouble here!" the Devil said. "Go away."

"What will I do?" Jack asked.

"Wander the earth," said the Devil.

"But it's dark! I can't see! How will I find my way?" Jack asked.

The Devil tossed Jack a burning coal. Jack put it inside a large turnip, so as not to burn his fingers. What a fine lantern!

People say Jack still walks around on earth carrying his lantern. And they call him Jack-of-the-Lantern, or Jack-o'-Lantern.

ACTIVITIES

1. The book, *Jack-o'-Lantern,* by Edna Barth, is a longer, yet modern retelling of the story of Jack and the Devil. You might want to read the book to your students.

2. Let the students make the story of Jack and the Devil into a book. Divide the story into parts. Give each part to a group of two or three students. Let the students work together to copy the text onto a sheet of construction paper and do some illustrations. Put all the sheets together to make a book.

3. Let the students see how many different words they can make from the letters in the words, "jack-o'-lantern" and "pumpkin."

4. Plan a field trip. Some ideas to consider are a trip to a farm to see pumpkins growing, a trip to the grocery store or pumpkin stand to buy pumpkins.

5. Teach a song about a jack-o'-lantern. See page 72.

6. Provide pictures of a pumpkin at various stages of growth. If you can't find such pictures, draw some simple charts to illustrate how pumpkins grow. Use these sketches to guide you. Use the charts as you discuss how pumpkins grow.

7. Provide a pumpkin for classroom use. Let the students help you make a jack-o'-lantern. Draw the face first, and leave the pumpkin uncut for several days. Then, cut into the pumpkin. Let students take turns cleaning out the seeds and the pulp. Then cut out the jack-o'-lantern features. Save the seeds. Roast some of them. (See page 48 for instructions on how to roast the seeds.)

8. Save the rest of the seeds until next spring. Let students plant them and watch them grow.

COSTUMES AND MASKS

by Ruth Shannon Odor

BACKGROUND

Whether its scary, pretty, or funny, putting on a costume and mask is part of our fun at Halloween.

It didn't use to be something you did just for fun. Long ago people really were afraid on October 31. If they had to go out after dark, they wore dark costumes and masks so the ghosts would not know who they were.

In the Middle Ages, people began to dress up to celebrate a new holiday, All Hallows' Day. They dressed up as angels or saints and marched around churches.

Our traditions of wearing costumes, masks, and "trick or treating" may come from Guy Fawkes Day festivities that were celebrated in England.

Guy Fawkes lived almost 400 years ago. He and others were angry at King James I. They plotted to kill him. When the men were caught, Guy was tortured and killed. Guy Fawkes Day became a time to remember him.

During the festivities on "Guy's day" people dressed up in costumes and went begging for "a penny for the Guy."

57

ACTIVITIES

1. Let students make costumes and masks. See pages 46-47 for some ideas.

2. When students have finished making their costumes and masks, let the children have a parade.

3. Let students write stories about the characters they are portraying in their costumes and masks. Younger students can dictate their stories to an aide.

4. Go to the library and find books that show pictures of masks. These could include masks made by the Iroquois Indians, by Northwest Coastal Indians, and by tribespeople in Africa, South America, or the Pacific Islands. Also find pictures of theatrical masks used in Greece, China, and other Asian countries. Let students browse through the books.

5. Help the children choose a favorite Halloween story, such as

"Wispy, the Littlest Witch" (see page 91). Let them plan how to tell the story as a play, make a list of props, and so forth. Talk about how important costumes are to a play. Let the children produce the play and put it on for their parents.

WITCH'S COSTUME

1. Let the students use black plastic bags to make dresses for the witches. (See sketches for ways to cut bags. Review the dangers of putting bags over the head.)

2. Each witch will need a hat. (See page 47.)

3. For a cape each child may cut a bag at the sides to make a long strip of black. Adjust the length by folding over one end of the bag. Punch holes at folded end. Add a draw string. Tie cape at neck.

4. Have the children make silver buckles by wrapping foil around cardboard buckles you have prepared in advance.

SLIT ONE SIDE ONLY

← ARM → HOLES

LEG HOLES

Punch holes at top: thread with black yarn. Draw closed for for ruffled neckline. Stuff bag to balloon skirt. Tie at waist with yarn belt.

"TRICK OR TREAT"

by Ruth Shannon Odor

BACKGROUND

The custom of going from door to door to say, "Trick or treat!" might be traceable back to any of several different beginnings.

In England people went from house to house on All Saint's Day begging for soul cakes. "A soul cake, a soul cake! A penny or a soul cake!" they cried.

Soul cakes were little square buns with currents in them. These sweetened rolls were baked in memory of people who had died. When people came begging for soul cakes, the residents of the houses would give soul cakes or money.

It was slightly different in Belgium. There children would stand beside little shrines built in front of their homes. They would beg for money from those who passed by to buy the cakes.

The way we "trick or treat" is much like an old Irish custom. On Halloween, groups of Irish people went from farm to farm asking for money or food. Sometimes the beggars wore masks. They said they were asking in the name of Muck Olla, an ancient Celtic god, or St. Columba, a monk. People thought something bad might happen if they didn't give something to the beggars. So they gave.

Some say "trick or treating" began in Europe in the 16th and 17th centuries. In that time, poor people, usually old women, went from door to door asking for food or money. People believed in witches then. If one of the women was turned away empty-handed, and something bad happened later—such as sickness or the death of a cow—people said the old woman put a curse on the house. They thought a bad *trick* had been played on them because they did not give a *treat*.

(Also see page 57.)

In America, in the 1800s, boys and girls would dress up as ghosts, goblins, or witches. They would have fun scaring the neighbors. Later, neighbors began to give children candy, gum, apples, and nuts. Today, children knock on doors and shout, "Trick or treat!"

ACTIVITIES

1. With the help of your students, compose a list: "Trick or Treating Safely"

(a) Go in the daytime, not after dark.

(b) Be sure an adult or older child goes with you.

(c) Be sure you can see through your mask.

(d) Bring home all the food; do not eat it on the way. Let a parent check it carefully before you eat it.

(e) Go only to the houses of people you know.

(f) Be careful crossing streets.

When the list is complete, make copies of it. Send a copy home with each student.

2. Some students might like to "trick or treat" for Unicef. Provide information for those students who wish to do this. Write to Unicef, The United Nations, New York, NY 10017, for information.

3. After Halloween, let students write stories about going "trick or treating." Younger students can dictate stories to an aide.

BOBBING FOR APPLES

by Ruth Shannon Odor

BACKGROUND

Bobbing for apples has been part of Halloween celebrations for many, many years. The country folk of England, Ireland, Scotland, and Wales were so afraid that ghosts and goblins were wandering about on Halloween night that they met together in groups in different homes.

As the people sat by the fire, they ate apples and nuts, told stories about ghosts, and played games. One game was bobbing for apples. If a boy could pick up an apple with his teeth, that meant the girl he loved would return his love.

ACTIVITIES

1. Older students may express a desire to try bobbing for apples. Provide a large tub. Fill it three-quarters full of water. Put apples in the water. Then let students take turns trying to bob for apples. To do this a person must kneel beside the tub and try to catch an apple in his mouth. He may not use his hands or arms. Make this voluntary.

2. Introduce your students to Johnny Appleseed. A good book to read to young students is *Johnny Appleseed,* by Gertrude Norman. It tells the story of John Chapman in a simple way. Older students would enjoy hearing you read from *Better Known as Johnny Appleseed,* by Mabel Leigh Hunt.

3. Have an apple-tasting party. Bring several varieties of apples to sample and compare as to size, taste, color. (Also see page 48.)

WITCHES AND BLACK CATS

BACKGROUND

People have talked about witches for a long, long time. In almost all parts of the world, people once believed in witches. Some people still do. They usually think of witches as men or women who can make good or bad things happen by using their magic.

Maybe you wonder how people thought up some of the ideas about witches we read in storybooks. It might have happened this way: Let's pretend. We are back in history, hundreds of years ago.

Imagine a poor, old, lonely woman. She lives all alone in a hut. She doesn't comb her hair very often. Sometimes she talks to herself, as some people do. She doesn't have any friends.

Let's suppose a black cat starts to hang around her hut, hoping to be fed. She feeds him. He stays.

It's night. You are on your way to your grandmother's house to see how she is. You pass the old woman's hut. Through her door, you see her stirring something in her soup pot. She's muttering to

herself. A broom leans against her wall.

You go a little way. The black cat darts across your path, shining its green eyes at you.

When you get to grandmother's house she is dead. You start to think about it. . .

You think: that old woman must be a witch. I saw her stirring something—her witch's brew.

"I knew it!" you say. "She turned into a cat and ran and killed my grandmother. Then she flew home on her broom."

(Our minds like to make patterns. People often connect things that happen with the things that happen before and after. This is a way many of us learn or remember.)

Sometimes the connections people make are just plain silly. And they are often wrong! Because an old woman likes cats and stirs her soup does not mean she is a witch who kills grandmothers. But for a time in history, some people made that same kind of wrong connection. They believed in witches— witches who could fly on brooms or could change themselves into animals, especially black cats.

Today, of course, we don't believe those things. But still we like to tell scary stories about witches. And at Halloween, we let the idea of Halloween witches remind us: it is much better to learn about the world and about ourselves than to go around being afraid of magic, cats, or storybook witches.

ACTIVITY—A WITCH

Materials: black and yellow construction paper, paste or glue, gray watercolor paint, straws, brushes.

Ahead of time, make one picture yourself, so you will know what to expect and be able to explain the process to students. Then, cut large circles from the yellow paper.

1. Give each student a piece of black construction paper and a yellow circle. Let students paste the circle to the page, to form a moon in a night sky.

2. Drip puddles of thin gray watercolor paint onto the bottom of the black paper. Let students blow through their straws to spread the gray paint in streaks and patterns over the black paper and yellow moon. This will end up looking a little like tree-top branches silhouetted against a night sky.

3. Let the paint dry. If you wish, make this a two-day project.

4. Give students brushes and more gray paint. Let each student paint a witch on a broomstick in the center or at the top of the picture. Students will be pleased with their paintings.

GHOSTS

BACKGROUND

Most early people believed in ghosts even if they didn't call them that. When the body died, the people wondered what happened to the "living" part of a person.

Some of them thought the spirit of the person would be angry that his body had died and would try to get revenge on those still living. Others thought the spirit would be lonely and would try to kill people so their spirits could join his. Many people buried food and valuable gifts with their dead people to help their spirits find their way to the other world and live well there. They didn't want any poor spirits staying around to haunt the village.

Today many people believe that the "soul" of a person continues to live after death, but few believe that ghosts really walk the earth.

It is true that spooky things happen sometimes—things that seemingly have no explanation. Experts study these things. Others just say, "It's a ghost."

Perhaps that is why old graveyards can be scary places on a dark night. . .old houses are thought of as being "haunted" and. . .people love to scare themselves with ghost stories and tales.

It all makes for shivery fun on a Halloween night!

ACTIVITY—GHOST STORIES

(For second grade and above)

On the chalkboard, draw a large ghost. *(See illustration.)* Add a simple frowning face. Be sure you leave lots of room for writing words in the ghost's flowing robe.

Ask students to help you fill up the ghost with scary words. Write all the words, as the students suggest them, on the ghost's robe. Don't stop until you have at least 20.

Let the students work in pairs to write ghost stories. Suggest that students include as many of the words as possible in their stories.

Tell students you will help them spell any words they want to use and don't know how to spell. Also instruct students to make their stories as crazy or zany as they want, or as scary as possible. Encourage their creativity.

You may want to read the stories aloud when students have finished them. Suggest that students listen for the words on the board.

After each story, find something to praise. Praise the zany or crazy parts, an especially scary part, a choice combination of words, or the number of words they used from the list on the board.

SPIDERS AND BATS
AND SCREECHING OWLS

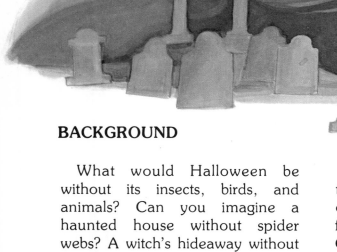

BACKGROUND

What would Halloween be without its insects, birds, and animals? Can you imagine a haunted house without spider webs? A witch's hideaway without bats? Or a scary night without an owl's spooky "Who-o-o?" These things are as much a part of Halloween as ghosts and witches.

In the daylight, in the zoo, by themselves, spiders, bats, and screeching owls are something to study—not spooky at all. But put them all together in the dark in an old deserted house, and it's enough to make even a witch's knees begin to tremble.

Spiders make a perfect addition to Halloween. Have you ever gone outside into the early morning and felt a spider's web on your face? Creepy! Don't you agree? And they like to spin those webs in old houses where the insect hunting is good. So of course they are always part of every haunted house scene.

And bats are rather frightening. Their shape is strange—with a tiny body and long, scalloped wings. Their faces are ugly, with large, large ears and sharp, sharp teeth. Bats often use dark caves or old barns for their homes. In the daytime, they hang upside down, with-

out moving; their wings, draped around them, look like witches' cloaks.

There really is no reason to fear bats, though it isn't a good idea to catch one. He might bite, and sometimes bats carry rabies. Maybe you have even heard people worrying that flying bats will get caught in their hair. As well as bats fly, that's not likely to happen. But insects should beware. Bats eat lots of them.

Another night creature, the owl, is also a symbol of Halloween. Screech owls, especially, have a terrible scary cry. People used to think it was a witch's cry. Screech owls hunt at night and sleep in the day. Owls, along with spiders and bats, are often pictured right along with witches in Halloween scenes.

Thus it is that spiders and bats and screeching owls are symbols of Halloween.

ACTIVITIES

1. Let students draw pictures of Halloween animals, birds, or insects. Display them.

2. Bring in books with photos or pictures of spiders, bats, and owls. Let the students look at them.

OWL MOBILE

Materials: brown, yellow, and black construction paper, scissors, yarn, glue, tape, paper punch.

1. Show children how to cut the top and bottom of an owl's face from a half sheet of brown construction paper (see sketch; perhaps you may want to duplicate the sketch on your chalkboard).

2. Let each child cut two large yellow eyes and a yellow triangle for a beak.

3. Each child will want to cut smaller black circles for eyes.

4. Each child will need four seven-inch pieces of yarn.

5. To assemble owl, first glue the black circles on the yellow ones. Then turn all the pieces over. Place top of head over bottom of head with space between. Place three pieces of yarn on top of head,

Fold bag in half vertically. Cut as illustrated.

"Sew" scallops together with tape.

Wear a dark shirt and pants.

reaching down to the bottom of head. Tape each end. Slip eyes and beak into position — one on each string and tape in back. Tape fourth piece of yarn to top of head and use as hanger. Turn owl over and watch him stare at you.

BE A BAT

Use the outline as a pattern for a bat mask. Have the children make costumes from black plastic bags as illustrated above.

HALLOWEEN IN SONGS AND POEMS

JACK-O'-LANTERN

Jane Belk Moncure   Paulette Lutz Glenn

Jack-o' lan-tern | shin-ing bright, | with a can-dle | for your light,

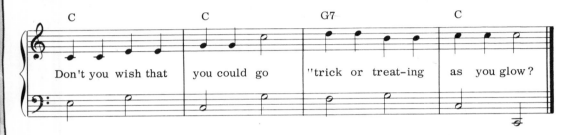

Don't you wish that | you could go | "trick or treat-ing | as you glow?

"TRICK OR TREAT"

Jane Belk Moncure   Paulette Lutz Glenn

"Trick or treat!" | "trick or treat!" | Give us some-thing

good to eat, And | we will skip on | down the street.

OWL-OW-EEN DAY

Jane Belk Moncure

Paulette Lutz Glenn

You may think it's Hal-low-een on Hal-low-een Day; But lit-tle owls think it's Owl-ow-een, and this is what they say:

(Spoken as chant)

"Whoo - oo? Who are you? This is Owl-ow-een Day!

Whoo - oo? Who are you? This is Owl-ow-een Day!"

MONSTERS

Jane Belk Moncure

Paulette Lutz Glenn

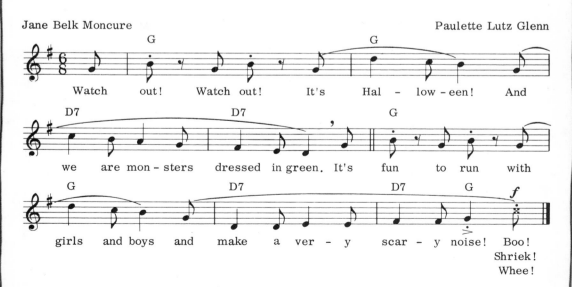

Watch out! Watch out! It's Hal - low - een! And we are mon - sters dressed in green. It's fun to run with girls and boys and make a ver - y scar - y noise! Boo! Shriek! Whee!

HALLOWEEN PARADE

by Paulette Lutz Glenn

Here is a simple chant for marching. You could use it when your students parade through the school in their Halloween costumes. If simple musical instruments are available, such as drums, sticks, triangles, and bells, let students use them as they chant. Otherwise, clap your hands to set the beat.

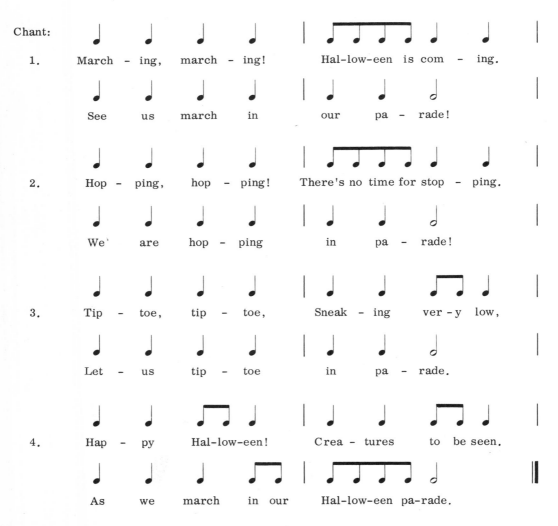

74

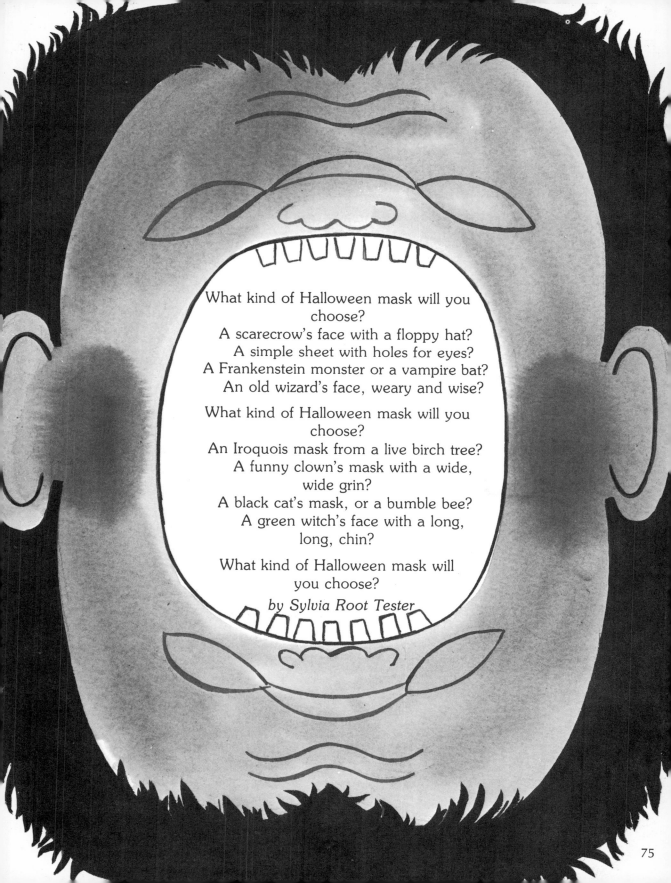

What kind of Halloween mask will you
choose?
A scarecrow's face with a floppy hat?
A simple sheet with holes for eyes?
A Frankenstein monster or a vampire bat?
An old wizard's face, weary and wise?

What kind of Halloween mask will you
choose?
An Iroquois mask from a live birch tree?
A funny clown's mask with a wide,
wide grin?
A black cat's mask, or a bumble bee?
A green witch's face with a long,
long, chin?

What kind of Halloween mask will
you choose?

by Sylvia Root Tester

HALLOWEEN VISITORS

by Gloria A. Truitt

I had the strangest visitors
   Last night at my front door.
First came a silent, spooky ghost. . .
   A long, white sheet he wore.
Then, next a witch in a black hat
   Stood cackling, with her broom.
I shook with fright, for I thought she might
   Fly right inside the room.
A monster with two heads knocked twice.
   I asked, "Who can this be?"
At once a little voice called out,
   "Are you afraid of me?"
I laughed to see a short, fat clown
   With flat and floppy feet,
Standing with a purple cat,
   Both yelling, "Trick or treat!"
I wonder where those strange things go. . .
   They simply disappear!
They only call on Halloween
   Which comes just once a year.

HALLOWEEN NIGHT

by Gloria A. Truitt

On Halloween night when the orange moon is out,
Ghosties and goblins go strolling about.
You might see a monster or warty ol' witch
Draped in rag-tatters the color of pitch.
You might hear a shriek or the shake of a shackle,
A clinkety-clank or a crackling cackle.
Watch closely and listen on this night of nights. . .
'Tis just once a year when you'll see such strange sights.
Then oddly these creatures flee home quick as lightning
And box up their sheets till next year's night of frightening!

LITTLE JACK PUMPKIN FACE

A Country Song

Little Jack Pumpkin Face
    Lived on a vine,
Little Jack Pumpkin Face
    Thought it was fine.

First he was small and green,
    Then big and yellow,
Little Jack Pumpkin Face
    Is a fine fellow.

HALLOWEEN POEM

by Dotti Hannum

I made a funny pumpkin face
    For everyone to see.
It looked so very big and cross,
    It even frightened me!

WITCH'S HELPERS

by Sylvia Root Tester

Black cat and blacker bat,
owl a-screeching in the tree,
eight-legged spider and legless snake —
these are the animals you see
helping a witch as she casts her spell;
and not a one of them will tell
the secret of her magic brew.
If you were a witch's helper. . .well. .
                would you?

THE WITCH
WITHOUT A BROOM

by Sandra Ziegler

On a night both dark and dreary
Sat a little ghost so weary
That a witch who happened by
Gave her broom to help him fly.

And since she didn't have her broom
She joined some "trick or treaters"
  in the gloom.
Who could tell on Halloween night
She really was a witch all right?

HALLOWEEN STORIES TO READ AND TELL

THE OLD WITCH

by Joseph Jacobs

Once upon a time there were two girls who lived with their mother and father. Father had no work. And the girls wanted to go away and seek their fortunes.

Now one girl wanted to be a servant, and her mother said she might if she could find a job. So she started for the town. Well, she went all about the town, but no one wanted a girl like her.

So she went on farther into the country, and she came to a place where there was lots of bread baking in an oven. The bread said, "Little girl, little girl, take us out, take us out. We have been baking

seven years, and no one has come to take us out."

So the girl took out the bread, laid it on the ground, and went her way.

Then she met a cow, and the cow said, "Little girl, little girl, milk me, milk me! Seven years have I been waiting, and no one has come to milk me."

The girl milked the cow, using some pails that stood near by.

Then she went on and came to an apple tree so loaded with fruit that its branches were almost breaking. The tree said, "Little girl, little

girl, help me shake the fruit from my branches."

And the girl said, "Of course I will, you poor tree." So she shook all the fruit off, propped up the branches, and left the fruit on the ground under the tree.

Then she went on again till she came to a house. Now in this house there lived a witch, and this witch took girls into her house as servants.

The witch told the girl what work she was to do. "You must keep the house clean and tidy, sweeping the floor and the fireplace; but there is one thing you must never do. You must never look up the chimney, or something bad will befall you."

So the girl promised to do as she was told. But one morning as she was cleaning, and the witch was out, she forgot what the witch had said. She looked up the chimney. When she did, a great bag of money fell down in her lap. This happened again and again. So the girl gathered up the money bags and started for home.

When she had gone some way, she heard the witch coming after her. She ran to the apple tree.

"Apple tree, apple tree hide me,
So the old witch can't find me;
If she does, she'll break my bones,
And bury me under the marble
  stones."

So the apple tree hid her. When the witch came up, she said:

"Tree of mine, tree of mine,
Have you seen a girl
With a willy-willy wag, and a
  long-tailed bag,
Who has stolen my money,
  all I had?"
And the apple tree said, "No, mother; not for seven years."

When the witch had gone down another way, the girl went on again. Just as she got to the cow,

she heard the witch coming after her. She ran to the cow.

"Cow, cow, hide me,
So the old witch can't find me;
If she does she'll break my bones,
And bury me under the marble
  stones."
So the cow hid her.

When the old witch came up, she said:

"Cow of mine, cow of mine,
Have you seen a girl
With a willy-willy wag, and a
  long-tailed bag,
Who has stolen my money,
  all I had?"
And the cow said, "No, mother, not for seven years."

When the witch had gone off another way, the little girl went on again. When she was near the oven, she heard the witch coming so she ran to the oven and cried:

"Oven, oven, hide me,
So the old witch can't find me;
If she does, she'll break my bones,
And bury me under the marble
    stones."

And the oven said, "I've no room; ask the baker." And the baker hid her behind the oven.

When the witch came up she looked here and there and everywhere, and then said to the baker:

"Man of mine, man of mine,
Have you seen a girl
With a willy-willy wag, and a
    long-tailed bag,
Who has stolen my money,
    all I had?"

So the baker said, "Look in the oven."

The old witch went to look, and the oven said, "Get in and look in the farthest corner."

The witch did so, and when she was inside, the oven shut her door, and the witch was kept there for a very long time.

The girl then went off again, reached her home with the money bags, married a rich man, and lived happily ever afterwards.

. . .

The other sister then thought perhaps she should go and do the same. So she went the same way. When she reached the oven, the bread said, "Little girl, little girl, take us out. Seven years have we been baking, and no one has come to take us out."

But the girl answered, "No, I don't want to burn my fingers."

So she went on till she met the cow, and the cow said, "Little girl, little girl, milk me, milk me, do. Seven years have I been waiting, and no one has come to milk me."

But the girl said, "No, I can't milk you; I'm in a hurry."

Then she came to the apple tree, and the apple tree asked her to help shake the fruit.

"No, I can't," said the girl.

She came to the witch's house and went to work. Like her sister—she forgot what she was told, and one day when the witch was out, she looked up the chimney, and down fell a bag of money. Well, she thought she would be off at once.

When she reached the apple tree, she heard the witch.

"Apple tree, apple tree, hide me,
So the old witch can't find me;
If she does, she'll break my bones,
And bury me under the marble
    stones."

But the tree didn't answer, and the girl ran on.

"Tree of mine, tree of mine,
Have you seen a girl
With a willy-willy wag, and a
    long-tailed bag,
Who has stolen my money,
    all I had?"

The tree said, "Yes, mother, she's gone down that way."

And as the witch went after the girl, the girl was heard to exclaim!

"Nowhere to hide, nowhere to
    hide
So the old witch can't find me."

With that, the old witch began to cackle her raucous laugh. The horrible sound so frightened the little girl that she dropped the money bag, and I'm told she's still running.

LAURIE HATED HALLOWEEN

by Penny Anderson

"Witches with broomsticks;
Goblins and ghosts;
   Black cats;
   Screeching bats;
These are the things
That scare me the most."

Laurie said the words over to herself. She could not get them out of her mind.

What really scared her the most was Halloween itself. How she hated it! She had hated it since she was four!

Laurie remembered that Halloween. She had been asleep in her bed when she heard a noise. She opened her eyes and saw. . .a ghost! She had screamed.

Then the lights had come on. Laurie had seen that the ghost was her mother. Mom had come from a Halloween party. She had not meant to frighten Laurie. She had just looked in to check on her.

Every Halloween since, Laurie had remembered that night. She knew it was silly. But, to her, Halloween meant a ghost in her room.

Now, Laurie looked in her mirror. She hated what she saw—a witch! She looked like a witch! Her tall black hat had rope hanging out

of it, like hair. The rope itched. So did her black dress and cape. Her pointed shoes hurt her feet.

And Laurie's mask was the worst part of all. It was wrinkled and green. The big hooked nose had a black wart on it.

Under her mask, Laurie's lip trembled. She looked awful!

"You look wonderful!" Mom said. Dad thought so too.

Mom gave Laurie her broom. "Remember, witches say, 'Double double, toil and trouble,' in their witch voices."

Laurie nodded.

Dad said, "You will like the haunted house. Halloween parties are fun. Come on! Let's go!"

She was glad she had on a mask,

even if she couldn't see out very well. Mom and Dad could not see in. They could not see her face.

Laurie stumbled to the car, dragging her broom behind her.

Dad helped Laurie out of the car at Mike's house, and led her to the door. It didn't look like Mike's house. There were cornstalks and pumpkins on the porch. The porch light was a jack-o'-lantern. Big black cats were painted on the window.

Laurie hung back as Dad walked up the steps. Before he touched the bell, the door opened.

A skeleton bowed.

"Have fun," Dad called to Laurie as he started back to the car. Laurie watched him go. A tear slid down her cheek inside her mask. She could not wipe it away. It tasted salty in the corner of her mouth.

A hand grabbed her arm. She spun around. It was the skeleton again. "Come in," he was saying.

The room was almost dark, except for jack-o'-lanterns. Black bats swung from the ceiling. Laurie had watched her mother make the bats. She knew they hung from strings. But they looked real. She shivered.

The room was filled with strange

creatures. They were all kids from her first grade. That made it worse. She knew the kids, but she didn't know who was under which costume.

A ghost stepped out of the corner. He waved his arms at Laurie. "Woooo. . . woooo. . .I just came out of a dead man's grave."

Laurie was so scared that she screamed and swung her broom at the ghost. He leaped into the air, laughing.

That ghost! He wasn't a ghost at all! He was Jeff. Laurie could see his new blue running shoes. It was Jeff all right.

As Laurie looked around the room, she recognized other children. The clown was Mary. Laurie could tell by her voice. The pirate was Joe. He was the tallest kid in the first grade. No costume could hide that.

Laurie laughed behind her mask. She wasn't scared anymore. She called out, "Double, double, toil and trouble." She was surprised to find that she sounded like the Wicked Witch of the West.

Laurie rode her broom around the room until the sketelon came in. He blew a blast on an orange Halloween horn. Everyone got quiet.

"Before we turn on the lights," he said, "we will have a contest. Move around the room. When you see someone you know, call out that person's name. If you are right, he or she must take off the mask. The last person still wearing a mask wins. Are you ready?"

"Yes!"

"Go!"

Laurie rode her broom across the room to the ghost. "Jeff!" she cried in her witch's voice.

"Aw, nuts! How did you know?"

Laurie laughed a witch's laugh.

"Mary!" she called to the clown, who had to pull off her mask.

Laurie guessed six people, but no one guessed who she was. She had

on witch's shoes. Her long hair did not show, and she remembered to use her witch's voice.

At last, Laurie was the only one left still wearing a mask.

"That has to be Laurie," Mary shouted above the noise. "She is the only one missing."

Laurie pulled off her mask and hat. The air felt cool of her face.

"You win the prize," said the skeleton. He pulled off his mask. It was Mike's dad.

He gave Laurie her prize—three guppies in a little bowl.

Dad was right, Laurie thought as she hugged her bowl of guppies. Halloween parties are fun.

WISPY, THE LITTLEST WITCH

by Rosemary Leahy Varney

Wispy, the littlest witch, was all a-tremble. Here it was, Halloween! Tonight would be the best night of the year. And maybe, just maybe, she would get to join the grown-up witches on their Halloween flight.

Wispy took the big gold key and unlocked the great black chest. She pushed open the top and reached in for her pointed black hat and long black cape. Wispy stretched for the black dress down in the bottom, and almost fell in. Finally, she took out the shiny black shoes with the magic silver buckles.

Quickly, Wispy ran to the big mirror and pulled the black dress over her head.

"I knew it would still be too big," said Wispy. The dress covered her hands and draped on the floor.

"Maybe the magic silver buckles will work anyway," she said.

Wispy turned around three times and whispered,

"Kiddlekazoo, klippity klee,
Magic buckles, fly for me!"

Nothing happened.

"These clothes are just too big for me," said Wispy. "That's why I can't fly."

Wispy looked for her box of safety pins. She pinned and pinned until the long black dress was up to her ankles.

Wispy pinned up the long black sleeves. Now they would not get in the way.

She stuffed newspapers in her black pointed hat. Now it would not fall down over her eyes.

She put on three pairs of thick socks. The black shiny shoes with the magic silver buckles almost fit.

"That ought to do it," said Wispy.

Wispy put on the cape and got her too-big broom.

"I'm late," whispered Wispy. "I should try the magic buckles again, but I don't have time."

Wispy ran as fast as she could to the meeting place in the woods. As she approached, Wispy heard the witches cackling and screeching.

"This year, we'll scare the cows on the Brown farm!"

"We'll swoop over the houses!"

"We'll haunt the graveyards!"

Suddenly, the witches saw Wispy. They snickered.

"Go home, Wispy," laughed one. "You couldn't scare anyone!"

"Who would be afraid of you," shrieked another, "with your clothes all pinned up like that?"

"You are so little," said a third. "I bet you can't even fly!"

Poor Wispy. A big tear squeezed out of her eye and dripped right down on her black dress.

The oldest witch raised her hand. All the other witches grew silent.

"Don't mind them," she said to Wispy. "Just try your magic buckles. If you are big enough, they will make you fly."

So Wispy turned around three times and whispered,

"Kiddlekazoo, klippity klee,
Magic buckles, fly for me!"

Slowly, Wispy started to rise in the air.

"Oh!" she gasped. "I don't think I like this! I don't like it at all!"

Just then, the shoes slipped off, and Wispy tumbled to the ground. The other witches cackled and shrieked.

"I'm sorry, Wispy," said the oldest witch, "but you really are too little to fly with us."

But then she asked, "Can you cook?"

Wispy's eyes sparkled, "Yes, that I can do," she said.

"We have no one to stir the soup while we are scaring people," said the oldest witch. "You can stay and watch the soup in our big cauldron. Be sure to stir it so it doesn't burn."

Wispy nodded happily. That was something even the littlest witch could do.

The black cats hopped on the brooms. One by one, the witches took off.

It grew darker and darker and quieter and quieter in the woods. Wispy stood and stirred the soup. She stirred and stirred, 'round and 'round. As she stirred, she got sleepier and sleepier. Finally, Wispy lay down on the ground and pulled her long black cape over her.

"Just a little rest," she said. "Then I'll stir the soup again."

"Wispy! Wispy!" called a squirrel. "Wake up! The soup boiled dry!"

Wispy jumped up and looked around. She smelled the burnt smell.

"Oh, dear," she wailed. She wanted to cry. "I'm too little for my clothes, too little to fly, too little to scare people, and now I'm too little to stay awake and stir the soup! The other witches will be back soon. Whatever will I do?"

But then she knew. Using her broomstick handle, she scratched a message in the dirt and hurried off.

"Where's Wispy?" the witches asked as they landed. "What happened to our soup? Phew! It smells horrible!" Then they saw Wispy's message.

"Wonder why she wants us to come to her cottage?" they asked each other as they hurried along.

"Something smells good," said the oldest witch.

"Come in, everybody," called Wispy. The witches shooed their cats into the yard where Wispy had put saucers of milk. Then they propped their brooms in the corner and sat down at the table.

Wispy had a big white apron tied around her to cover her black dress. There was flour on her shiny black shoes, and her hat was tipped over her ear.

She carried steaming bowls of Blackwitch Stew to the table. Then she filled mugs with hot and spicy Cider Brew.

The witches were tired and hungry. They ate and ate. Wispy kept bringing more bowls of steaming Blackwitch Stew and filling the mugs with the hot Cider Brew.

Finally, Wispy brought in a great heaping platter of cookies, cut in cat shapes and hat shapes and bat shapes.

"Wispy," said the the oldest witch, "you may be too little for your clothes, too little to fly, and too little to scare people. But you surely can cook!"

The other witches rubbed their stomachs and agreed.

"Well, then, witches," continued the oldest witch, "I have an idea. Let's make Wispy our Halloween cook. During every busy Halloween, Wispy can cook for us."

"A good idea," they agreed.

"A great idea," said Wispy. Even though I'm little, I can cook. Besides, flying is scary."

"Well, then, it's all settled. And now we must go, Wispy. Soon the moon will disappear and the sun will be up. Thank you for the delicious food. We'll see you next Halloween."

"Good-bye, good-bye," called Wispy as they flew away.

Wispy smiled as she took off her long black dress and put it in the big black chest. She smiled as she dropped in the shiny black shoes with the magic silver buckles, the black cape, and finally the big black hat stuffed with newspapers. Then Wispy locked the chest and put the gold key under her pillow. She was still smiling when she crawled into her little bed. For now, she was truly a Halloween witch.

TEENY-TINY

by Joseph Jacobs

This is a story that is GUARANTEED to scare you!

Once upon a time there was a teeny-tiny woman who lived in a teeny-tiny house in a teeny-tiny village. Now, one day this teeny-tiny woman put on her teeny-tiny bonnet and went out of her teeny-tiny house to take a teeny-tiny walk. And when this teeny-tiny woman had gone a teeny-tiny way, she came to a teeny-tiny gate. So the teeny-tiny woman opened the teeny-tiny gate, and went into a teeny-tiny graveyard.

And when this teeny-tiny woman had got into the teeny-tiny graveyard, she saw a teeny-tiny bone on a teeny-tiny grave. And the teeny-tiny woman said to her teeny-tiny self, "This teeny-tiny bone will make me some teeny-tiny soup for my teeny-tiny supper."

So the teeny-tiny woman put the teeny-tiny bone into her teeny-tiny pocket and went home to her teeny-tiny house.

Now when the teeny-tiny woman got home to her teeny-tiny house, she was a teeny-tiny bit tired. So she went up her teeny-tiny stairs to her teeny-tiny bed, and put her teeny-tiny bone into a teeny-tiny cupboard. And when this teeny-tiny woman had been asleep a teeny-tiny time, she was awakened by a teeny-tiny voice from the teeny-tiny cupboard, which said:

"Give me my bone!"

And this teeny-tiny woman was a teeny-tiny bit frightened, so she hid her teeny-tiny head under the teeny-tiny covers and went to sleep again.

And when she had been asleep again a teeny-tiny time, the teeny-tiny voice again cried out from the teeny-tiny cupboard a teeny-tiny bit louder,

"GIVE ME MY BONE!"

This made the teeny-tiny woman a teen-tiny bit more frightened, so she hid her teeny-tiny head a teeny-tiny bit further under the teeny-tiny covers. And when the teeny-tiny woman had been asleep again a teeny-tiny time, the teeny-tiny voice from the teeny-tiny cupboard said again, a teeny-tiny bit louder,

"GIVE ME MY BONE!"

And this teeny-tiny woman was a teeny-tiny bit more frightened. But . . . she put her teeny-tiny head out of the teeny-tiny covers, and said in her teeny-tiny voice,

(Shout) **"TAKE IT!"**

(Pause.) There now, weren't you scared?